THE MIRACLE OF
THE
AL-QUR'AN

THE MIRACLE OF THE QUR'AN

First published in Malaysia by
Tertib Publishing
23-2 Jalan PJS 5/30
Petaling Jaya Commercial City (PJCC)
46150 Petaling Jaya, Selangor
Malaysia

Tel: +603 7772 3156

First Edition: January 2020

Cover design: Muhamad Aidil Abdul Wahab
Transcription: Hanis Hanani Mohammad Tahir
Typesetting & Layout: Ainul Syuhada
Printed by: Firdaus Press Sdn. Bhd.

CONTENTS

Preface

The Miracle of the Qur'an. The Qur'an is the greatest miracle of God (Allah) and the Qur'an is the proof of the truthfulness of Islam. It is the standing and everlasting miracle, but very rarely, have we heard how is it a miracle?

The Qur'an is the ultimate miracle of our Prophet Muhammad (Sallahualaihi wassalam – S.A.W). It is such a miracle that all the other miracles are considered trivial and inconsequential compared to the Qur'an. This is because the Qur'an is so powerful, so bright and blinding that no matter how bright the other miracles are; when you have the sun, the stars become useless.

In this book, Dr. Yasir Qadir discussed on the miracles of the Qur'an that we either have never acknowledged or we often overlooked. The miracles of the Qur'an are endless and the points are abundance to be mentioned.

THE QUR'AN AS A *MU'JIZAH*

We began by praising Allah (Subhanahu wa ta'ala – S.W.T) by sending *salam* on the Prophet Muhammad S.A.W. Now as Muslims, we all know that the Qur'an is the greatest miracle of Allah S.W.T. It is something that has been taught as children and we say it almost to all of our Non-Muslim friends.

Most of us have even heard many lectures by many eloquent speakers and many academics who keep on telling us the Qur'an is the greatest miracle of God and the Qur'an is the proof of the truthfulness of Islam. The Qur'an is the standing and everlasting miracle, but very rarely, have we heard how is it a miracle? And what is the whole concept of this miracle? This book will discuss on this matter to elucidate on what is the very concept of God-sending miracles, why and how is the Qur'an a miracle?

Now the concept of miracle in Arabic is called a *mu'jizah* and it means something that which cannot be imitated. A *mu'jizah* means that which cannot be done again. It is something that is supernatural that breaks the natural laws that we are accustomed to. It is a concept so profound, deep, and unintelligible to the average mind of a human being. The only explanation that any rational person can come to is that this is a miracle from God Himself. The example of these miracles are many. In fact, every single prophet that Allah S.W.T has sent, was sent with miracles.

For example, the simplest one is Prophet Musa (Alaihi Salam – A.S). The Prophet Musa A.S.; look at his miracles that Allah gave him. Allah S.W.T gave him nine miracles. Allah says in the Qur'an in Surah Al-Isra: Verse 101. Nine miracles. One of the miracles was this staff that was when Musa threw it, it becomes into a snake. This is not something that any human being could do. Another miracle of Prophet Musa A.S is the parting of the Red Sea; now who can possibly hit the Red Sea with a staff and the Red Sea parts into two? This is something that is above and beyond the explanation of any human being.

The Prophet Jesus Christ – The Prophet Isa Ibn Maryam. He was given miracles upon miracles. His very birth was a miracle that has never ever been replicated to this day and it can never be replicated. His very birth from a virgin lady; his mother Maryam A.S – This is a miracle. The fact that he predicted so many things that he told the people of Isrāil – He told the children of Israel "I will tell you what is in your houses right now" and he told them.

The fact that he resurrected the dead before their very eyes. Allah S.W.T told him to call out such a person's name who had just been buried and Prophet Isa A.S called out the name and Allah S.W.T brought the dead person back to life. The person was clinically dead; he was completely dead, not a false death that happens to this day. He was dead and his spirit has been taken away but Allah S.W.T returned his spirit to him and resurrected him back to life.

Other than the miracles of Prophet Isa A.S that have been mentioned above, he created a pigeon from clay and he blew into it. Allah S.W.T then caused life to be blown into the pigeon and so from clay, Allah created life as He has created the life of man. These are what we call miracles. Now why does Allah

S.W.T send miracles? What is the purpose of sending miracles?

The purpose of sending miracles is to prove that such and such a person is The Messenger of God. This is the purpose of a miracle. The reason why Allah S.W.T sends miracles is to show mankind that this person is not a liar, he is not a fraud nor a charlatan. He is indeed somebody whom I (Allah) am helping and I will prove this help to you (prophet) in a manner that will be beyond the shadow of a doubt. Miracles manifest itself as being directly from God.

THE CHALLENGE OF THE QUR'AN

When our Prophet Muhammad S.A.W came, the Quraish also demanded miracles as well. They said to Prophet S.A.W "Why don't you cause the angels to come down? Why don't you split up the earth and cause rivers to flow in this barren land of Makkah? Why don't you make this desert into a green area?" They wanted miracles and so Allah S.W.T gave them miracles. He gave them many miracles, but he gave them the ultimate miracle as well and that is the miracle of The Qur'an.

In five different verses, Allah issues a challenge and these verses are called the verses of challenge; in five separate and distinct verses, Allah issues a challenge and one of these verses is Allah saying in the Qur'an, Say:

> "If the mankind and the Jinn came together
> in order to produce something similar to the
> Qur'an, they would not be able to produce it,
> even if they helped one another."

> (Surah Al-Isra': Verse 88)

The first revelation of verses of challenge Allah says "Bring forth a Qur'an similar to it. If you think this book is a fraud, why don't you do the same?" This is a challenge and they plotted, plan but they could not meet up this challenge. So Allah S.W.T reduced the challenge and He said "Why don't you bring forth only 10 surahs? Not the whole Qur'an. Why don't you bring forth 10 surahs that are fabricated and forged? See if you can imitate the Qur'an." They could not even do this. They couldn't do ten.

Allah then reduced the challenge again from the entire Qur'an, to 10 surahs, Allah reduced it again and He issued the ultimatum and this is the final of the five verses revealed. The final of the five verses is found in the Surah Al-Baqarah, Allah S.W.T says "And if you all are in doubt about what I have revealed to My servant, bring a single chapter like it." (Surah Al-Baqarah: Verse 23). Not the whole Qur'an. Not 10, Allah reduced the challenge.

Notice how this is a further indication of the miraculous nature of the Qur'an. The challenge is issued high "Bring forth the whole Qur'an", they cannot do it. So Allah lowers it, "Bring forth 10 surahs". They could not do it. Allah lowers it even more "Bring forth only one surah". Then Allah gives the ultimatum, Allah said,

"Call whomever you want" then Allah says "But if you do not (succeed in the challenge) - and you will never be able to."

(Surah *Al-Baqarah*: Verse 24).

It is the ultimatum and another miracle because it is a prediction. Allah says but if we cannot do it and then there is a phrase that is put in brackets in English "very surely, you will never be able to do it." If we cannot do it, it is a condition, but then there is a prediction we will never be able to do it. Until the end of times, we will not do it. We can't do it, and we will never be able to do it. Then be prepared to face the punishment of Allah, of fire whose fuel are stones and men.

Now this ultimatum to produce a surah similar to the Qur'an, it is a standing ultimatum that is in existence until right now. Up until this time, we are allowed to issue the same challenge, not just to our opponent, not just to our debater, but to all of mankind. We challenge mankind and we say "O mankind who has disbelieved in the Qur'an! Come together, all of you. All of your scientists, your computers, your program managers, come together. All of you! Write computer codes, see if you can do it. Do whatever you want, bring your poets, bring your noble laureates of the Arabic language. Do whatever you want and bring forth; not the whole Qur'an, not even 10 surahs. Bring forth one surah like the Qur'an, if you are truthful and your claim that the Qur'an is not from God."

THE QU'RAN ECLIPSED OTHER MIRACLES

Now the question that arises is, what is the status of the Qur'an's miracle that vis-à-vis the other miracles that Prophet Muhammad S.A.W was given? The Prophet Muhammad S.A.W was given many miracles. We know he was given so many miracles. One of the miracles that he was given was the fact that he split the moon in half.

"The Day of Judgment has come close and the moon has been split (in two)."

(Surah *Al-Qamar*: Verse 1).

This is a miracle. Prophet Muhammad S.A.W pointed to the moon when the Quraish challenged him to split it in half. The moon then splits in half right in front of their eyes.

Of his many miracles was that on numerous occasions "I witnessed account" (by the companions of Prophet S.A.W), he took a small quantity of food and he caused it to suffice for hundreds, sometimes thousands. In the Battle of The Trench, one glass of milk was drunk by over 1500 companions to their fill. Each one drinking to his fill! More than 1500 people drank from one cup of milk and all of the people reported this.

In the Battle of Hudaibiyah, one canister of water suffice the entire army of 1400 people; not just to drink, but to do wudhu' as well. They did wudhu' and they drank from one canister of water. On so many occasions, there is only small quantities of food in the Battle of Tabuk, a few dates and few pieces of bread were brought in front of the Prophet S.A.W. He was told this is all the whole army has. That is all they had! So he dipped his hands in it and he prayed to Allah S.W.T and that one plate of food sufficed for the entire army of Tabuk. This is a living miracle. People saw it, people reported it and there are many more besides these.

The question is though, what is the relative status of the miracle of The Qur'an vis-à-vis the other miracles that he was given? The response is, the Quran is the ultimate miracle of our Prophet Muhammad S.A.W. It is such a miracle that all the other miracles are considered trivial and inconsequential compared to the Qur'an. In comparison to the Qur'an, all of the other miracles become inconsequential. This is because the Qur'an is so powerful, so bright and blinding that no matter how bright the other miracles are; when you have the sun, the stars become useless. There are stars, beautiful and magnificent, but when the sun comes out, of what use are the stars.

The Prophet S.A.W. was given numerous miracles, there is one miracle that eclipsed all the other miracles and that is the miracle of the Qur'an. We know this by many verses in a hadith, and of a hadith which shows us the miracles of the Qur'an. Hadith Sahih Al-Bukhari, that the Prophet S.A.W said, Allah has sent prophets and given them miracles. So the general rule, miracles are not only for Prophet S.A.W. Allah has sent prophets and given them miracles because of which the people believed in him. This is why the people believed in the prophets, because of the miracles.

He (Prophet Muhammad S.A.W.) said, "The only miracle that I have been given". He said "the only" even though he was given more. He is saying "the only" because this one miracle is so grand, so magnificent that all the other miracles are inconsequential compared to it. Prophet S.A.W said "The only miracle that I have been given, is the revelation that Allah has sent down to me. This Qur'an. That is my only miracle." Then he said, "And because of it, I hope to have the largest quantity of followers on The Day of Judgement. Because of this miracle, I want my ummah to be the biggest ummah."

What does that show? What does that tell us? It tells us that the miracle of the Qur'an is so great that it even eclipses all of the miracles of all of the prophets before the coming of Prophet Muhammad S.A.W. He said because of this one miracle, he wished to have the largest followers. What does that mean? It means that this miracle is so powerful, it is so clear and perspicuous of itself that he doesn't need anything else to cause him to have more followers than all of the other prophets before him.

So powerful is the miracle. So potent is the force of Qur'an, that the Qur'an will make his ummah the largest quantity of followers on The Day of Judgement. And that is the truth, is it not? Prophet S.A.W. has the largest of all ummahs when we look at the quantity and quality of practicing people, practicing believers. Not just somebody who says in a book "I am a Muslim/Christian". Somebody who actually believes and prays. There is no question that in terms of actual practice, there are far more practicing Muslims than there are in other religion on the face of this Earth. The Qur'an gives us faith and stability. It makes us true believers unlike somebody who says "I am a Christian or Jew" and he doesn't necessarily believe in that faith.

THE POWER OF THE QUR'AN

The Qur'an is the ultimate miracle of the Prophet S.A.W. Now the question arises, how and why is the Qur'an the ultimate miracle? The response to that is, that all of the other miracles of the prophets that were before the Prophet S.A.W, were temporary miracles! Have we seen the splitting up of the Red Sea? Did anybody witness that? Were any of us there? Nobody was there, correct? Did anybody witness the resurrection done by Jesus Christ? No. Did they happened? Yes. How do we know? We believe. We weren't there. Even the other miracles of the Prophet S.A.W.; the splitting of the moon, did we see it? No. So those miracles were miracles to those who saw them. As for those who come after them, we must simply believe. Imaan bi al-Ghayb (The Faith of the Unseen).

Now, the miracle of the Qur'an it removes the time space factor from the miracle. We don't have to have been in Arabia in the 7th century to see this miracle. We can be in India in the 21st Century, we can be in America in the 25th century and we can still see the miracle of the Qur'an. The miracle of the Quran removes the time space constraint of the miracles and that is why the miracle of the Qur'an is called

The Eternal Miracle, The Everlasting Miracle. It is the miracle that we can touch, we can feel, we can see, we can recite. These are a miracle; our senses can attest to. Unlike any other miracle. So when the miracle is so powerful that breaks the constraints of time and place that it becomes an eternal and universal miracle then that is the ultimate miracle and this is the miracle our Prophet Muhammad S.A.W has been given.

In another indication of the power of the miracle of the Qur'an; look at the miracles of the other prophets. The miracles of the other prophets. Look at Prophet Musa A.S, he was given the miracle of the hand coming out and light comes out of it. The miracle of the staff thrown and becoming a snake. What was the purpose of this? So that they believe in The Message. What was The Message? The Book. The Taurah. So the miracles proved The Message. Correct?

As for Prophet Isa A.S, what happened? Same thing. Here are the miracles, I (Allah) want you to believe in The Message. Here are the miracles, this is the message. What happened with the miracle of Prophet Muhammad S.A.W? As for the other books.

The Taurah, The Injil, The Zabur, they needed these miracles to support it. They needed these miracles to tell the people that this book, is a Book of God. But the miracle of the Qur'an is that it does not need supporting evidence.

The miracle and the Qur'an had been combined in one revelation and the revelation is the miracle, the miracle is The Book; The Book is not in need of supporting evidence. It is the evidence and the message combined in one. What other miracle do we leave with The Qur'an? The miracle of The Qur'an is so powerful that it does not need any other miracles to prove it. This is why The Qur'an is such a powerful miracle.

Two factors have been mentioned that demonstrate the power of the miracle of the Qur'an. The first of them removing the time space factor. Removing geographic location, removing an era, a year. We don't have to have been alive in 620 C.E. or 10 Hijrah to have witnessed the miracle of the Quran and we don't have to be in The Arabia. It can be appreciated by all of mankind. The second factor, the miracle is not in need of another miracle. The Book is not in need of supporting evidence. The evidence is the miracle, the miracle is the evidence all combined in one and that is the ultimate miracle which has made the Qur'an so powerful.

THE ELOQUENCE OF THE QUR'AN

The question still remains how is it miraculous? The reason has been said, but what and how is it a miracle? Now somebody says, "Okay, fine, I understand the concept and theory, but show me miracle. Will the Qur'an speak to me from the book? What is the miracle? Show me. Explain to me." This we get to how the Qur'an is miraculous. How the Qur'an is miraculous is a very long topic but we will summarize them into a few points.

The first manner of which The Qur'an is miraculous is the language and style of the Qur'an. The sheer eloquence of the Qur'an above that of any human's speech. It is the unique arrangement, the organization of the surah and verses. The manner of which the words are arranged. The choice of words that are use, the choice of synonyms that are used. The precision with Allah S.W.T speaks in the Qur'an. Looking at the Qur'an and reading the Qur'an, it is clear it is not the speech of men, it is the speech of God. This is something that even the Arabs of old appreciated it directly. There are numerous stories of people whom The Prophet S.A.W recited the Qur'an to. They were so amazed at its recitation that they knew that this was not of men's.

The best example for this is the greatest poet of the Arabs. The greatest poet of the Arabs, his name was Al-Waleed Ibn 'Utbah, he was their living Shakespeare, he was their most knowledgeable and most sophisticated poet. Al-Waleed Ibn 'Utbah agreed to negotiate with the Prophet Muhammad S.A.W and he went up to him and he began conversing with him and he said "O Muhammad S.A.W! You have broken our ranks and brought forth something new. You have destroyed our old ways, ridiculed our forefathers. Why don't you stop this message of yours and I will give you anything that you want. I will give you as much money as you want. I will help you marry any woman that you want. I will make you the leader of the Arabs but stop this preaching of Islam. The Prophet S.A.W said, "Have you finished?" He said "Yes".

The Prophet S.A.W said "Then listen to me" and he continued reciting. Can we just imagine hearing a recitation of the Qur'an, how beautiful was it? Imagine if we could witness the recitation of the Prophet Muhammad S.A.W, what voice did he had? What voice do we think Allah blessed him with? And he recited the Qur'an in tilawah and he recited and recited until finally a verse came which said "and of you refuse The Messenger now, then await the punishment of Allah that will come like a bolt of thunder." (Surah Fussilat: Verse 1-13).

Waleed Ibn 'Utbah was listening and as he was listening he gets more and more scared, trepidation, fear when this verse was recited. He stood up, he jumped, he puts his hand on the mouth of Prophet Muhammad S.A.W he said, "I begged you by Allah, stop!" he turned his back and ran away thinking the bolt of lightning will come right there and then smack him out of his existence. The power of the Qur'an was so powerful, he ran back to the Quraish, The Quraish said to him when they saw him, they said "This man who has come is not the same man who has left us.

Something has happened in the meantime. So when Al-Waleed Ibn 'Utbah came back, he said "O my people, you all know that I am the best poet amongst you, nobody can win me in a competition of poetry. But wallahi this speech that I just heard, it is not the speech of men. Not even the speech of Jinn. This is not even the speech of Jinn. This message he said, it has a sweetness that I cannot described. It has a power, an aura that is beyond human understanding.

Waleed Ibn 'Utbah said "Leave this man alone, for this verily this speech, shall conquer all of the Arabs". This speech, The Qur'an will conquer all of the Arabs. This Al-Waleed Ibn 'Utbah testified that he knows poetry; this is not poetry. He knows the speech of men, this is not the speech of men. And the Quraish rejected him and ridiculed him (prophet S.A.W.) and Al-Waleed as well and they continued in their arrogance against the Prophet S.A.W. There many other instances of this nature and of course, this is the type of miracle that we must understand Arabic, to fully appreciate.

To this day, Arabs of all different religion and many people think all Arabs are Muslims; this is not true. There are Arabs who are atheist and secular, there are many Arabs, millions who are Christians. There used to be Arabs who are Jews as well. Arabs are actually of many different ethnicities and religion. It's not just one tribe and one religion. It is a universally agreed fact amongst all the speakers of the Arabic language. Regardless of their religion, that the ultimate perfection of the Arabic language is the language of the Qur'an. It is called the classical standard Arabic. Nothing is better than the Qur'an; even they acknowledge this.

This is something that has been testified if we have spoken to them, they have told us "Yes, we know that the standard of Arabic is The Qur'an." They understand this, but they simply refuse to believe it is from God. "Maybe he (The Prophet S.A.W.) was a talent poet" they say. Exactly what the Qur'an said, "But they refuse to acknowledge it is from God" nonetheless this is the type of miracle that even the basic speaker of Arabic will appreciate and we must learn Arabic to understand this facet of the miracle.

THE PROPHECIES
IN THE QUR'AN

There are many types of other miracle as well which we don't need to understand Arabic to appreciate. Of the types of miracle, the Qur'an has come with many predictions of things that will happen in the future and these predictions have come true and the greatest type of example of this type of prediction is that in a certain battle that the Romans would win over the Persians.

At the time of the Prophet S.A.W. there were two superpowers, the Roman (Byzantine) Empire and the Persian (Sassanid) Kingdom. They were the two superpowers of the time and continuously fighting and waging war for over 300 years. A certain time came during the reign of Heraclius in the Romans side and Khosrow Parviz in the Persian side where for some reason, the Romans withered and dwindled. And their power waned. The Persians solidify and consolidated where their power waxed and increased. So much so that when they had a battle, the Persians won the greatest victory for centuries over the Romans.

It was predicted that the Roman Empire would collapse. It was on the verge of death at that time. The people thought that's it now that it is only a matter of time where Persia will completely wipe off Rome from the face of this Earth. At that point in time and all time low, Allah revealed in the Qur'an,

> "Alif lam meem, the Romans have been defeated. In a land nearby but it's only a matter of time. After this defeat, that they shall be the victors." In only a few years, this is because all the matters belong to Allah. From the beginning to the end. All matters belong to Allah and the decree by Allah.

(Surah Ar-Rum: Verse 1-4)

Now the question is, this verse is in the future tense. It begins in the past, the Romans have been defeated. Factual statement but then it immediately moves to the future tense. "But after this defeat, they will in the future be victorious and indeed." (Surah Ar-Rum: Verse 3). When this verse was revealed, it was so certain that they would not be victorious they were so clear about this that Ubay Ibn Khalaf; one of the leaders of the Quraish made a bet with Abu Bakr and he said "I will bet you 100 camels that the Romans will not win over the Persians in the next war" and indeed it so happened that in seven year time Allah S.W.T. caused the Romans to win a resounding victory.

The night before the battle, the royal Persian family entered into a civil war. Uncle fought with nephew, cousin fought with cousin, brother in law fought with sister in law, they fell into civil war, in the royal family. Due to this large factions, the unity split away that they fought. Few days before the Romans side of the attack, the Romans managed to form alliances with other nations that they never thought would happen and so the Romans managed to get extra troops. The Persians loss what they had of the troops. What happened? The Romans Heraclius II won the biggest victory over Khosrow Parviz in recent history and Allah predicted this in the Qur'an and it is a prediction for all to see until this day. There are other predictions in the Qur'an as well.

THE ACCURACY OF THE QUR'AN

The Qur'an is full of stories of the previous prophets and nations. It mentioned Fir'aun, it mentioned Haman, it mentioned Thamud, and it mentioned Moses, Jesus and Mary. It mentioned all types of stories. The stories of the Arabs and the stories of other than the Arabs. Now most people don't understand and realise this point, but when the Prophet S.A.W. was in Makkah, there was no library in all of the Arabia Peninsular. The people in Makkah were illiterate and backward nation. They couldn't read, they couldn't write. They didn't have libraries.

People at the time of Prophet S.A.W. did not know the details of these stories. They didn't know them. It is as if in our time, imagine there is no internet and television, or even in tribes that do not have them. Suppose somebody living in the safari of Africa or the Aboriginals of Australia. Completely cut off from society and he has no access and we know this for a fact that all of the sudden he starts spouting forth the histories of Rome and Persia. The histories of the Muslim world, The Ottomans and The Mughals.

Out of nowhere, comes an educated man, a cultured, civilized human being who knows the histories of previous nations. How was this possible? He doesn't have a library, he doesn't have access to knowledge. None of the people around him are aware of this fact and yet he comes forth with crystal clarity informs us of Fir'aun and Musa. He informs us of Isa and Maryam, He informs us of Adam and Hawa, He informs us the Kings of Namrud and all of these societies. Where did this come from? Allah S.W.T. reveals in The Qur'an,

> "These stories are from the knowledge of The Unseen that We reveal to you. Neither you nor the people before you were aware of these stories."

(Surah Hud: Verse 49).

This is the miracle of The Qur'an and notice as well how precise The Qur'an is in these stories. For example, in the time of Prophet Yusuf A.S., the Pharaohs of Egypt were expelled by an outside dynasty. Right before the coming of Yusuf A.S., those Pharaohs were expelled by a foreign and invading force. Egypt was ruled by a line of kings that were not Pharaohs and this was well known historically speaking. So therefore to call them

Pharaohs would be a mistake, but when we look at the Old Testament and we see the story of Joseph, it refers to the ruler of Egypt as the Pharaoh, but he was not a Pharaoh, to that family, he never called himself a Pharaoh. It was a different dynasty all together when The Qur'an talks about the story of Yusuf A.S. what does it say?

In reference to the story of Prophet Yusuf A.S in Surah Yusuf, the verses will say, "And the Malik (means King in Arabic) saw, and the Malik dreamt"; Al-Malik, The King and when it talked about Musa, go to Fir'aun. When it talked about Yusuf, Allah S.W.T. says The Malik said "Bring him to me." (Surah *Yusuf*: Verse 50). This precision of telling a story, it is inhumanly impossible that he Prophet S.A.W was aware of these facts up until recent time that people would call the rulers of Egypt all Pharaohs, but technically that is not correct. They were not Pharaohs for only 150 years, they were not Pharaohs. In that time, Yusuf's story occurred and so Allah does not call them Pharaohs. He calls them 'king'.

THE PERFECTION OF THE QUR'AN

The Qur'an contains the laws and beliefs in it as a source of guidance. In other words, The Message of the Qur'an. The fact that the Qur'an comes with such a beautiful theology. Look at the theology of the Qur'an and compare it to Christianity, Buddhism and Hinduism. The theology of the Qur'an is logical and rational. It appeals to the sense of man, there is one God, All Perfect, worship him alone; simple. Look at any other religion, there will be soap opera; drama. We will see a human mind and a human product writing a story down.

Similarly the laws of Islam. Laws of marriage and divorce, laws of inheritance, the laws of the Shariah, they are the all perfect law. And that is the topic of many lectures which many people have spoken to about women in Islam, justice in Islam, the legal system in Islam. All of these law demonstrates the miracle of The Qur'an and bringing these laws compare this to any of human's constitution and we will find contradiction. Anybody who studies human law will testify how ridiculous human law is. How many loopholes there are? How many contradictory there are? How many laws there are?

Any person who studies constitutional law will tell us every constitution has to be updated. Laws have to be changed. What is allowed one year, will become prohibited in the next. What is prohibited in one year, will become allowed in the next. In the American constitution there was been so many amendment. One year alcohol is prohibited, one year it is allowed. We cannot compare this to The Qur'an. The eternal, pure, unchanging immutable laws of The Qur'an. This too is a miracle that can be appreciated by friend and foe, by Arabs and non-Arabs, by Muslims and by non-Muslims.

THE SCIENTIFIC MIRACLES IN THE QUR'AN

Yet another miracle of the Qur'an is the issue of the scientific miracles in the Qur'an. The fact that Allah mentions facts and points in the Qur'an that were humanly impossible to know at the time and era of the Prophet Muhammad S.A.W and all of us are familiar with some of the examples of these. The clearest example in most of our minds is the description of the human embryo. How Allah describes the evolution of the human embryo.

From the sperm and zygote. From the small tingling thing Allah calls the child in the womb that which 'hangs' (Surah *Al-Alaq*). No human being knew that an embryo hangs from the womb of the mother. Nobody knew this until 300 years ago. Allah S.W.T calls it that which hangs; it's a hanging thing because it is clinging to the womb of a mother. Allah S.W.T calls an embryo that creation which, "We created in three veils of darkness," (Surah *Az-Zumar*: Verse 6) and if we look at the layers of the embryo, there are literally three separate layers that separate the embryo from the outside world. So many precise things in the Qur'an.

Allah says in the Qur'an, "We have sent down iron" (Surah *Al-Hadid*: Verse 25). Earth is the only planet that we know of that has iron to this quantity. Iron is not a product according to the modern day scientists. It is something that the scientists cannot explain; where did it come from on Earth. A large percentage of the Earth is iron. The latest theory says that iron was formed by meteorites coming in at a certain point in time before the earth solidified. Meteorites came in and the iron was implanted inside the Earth, because iron was not created from the fusion of helium and hydrogen.

Iron is not a byproduct of other things that the sun possibly can create through nuclear fusion. Iron was that which we don't know where it came from. Allah says out of all of the elements, Allah mentions this one element and He says as for iron, "We sent it down", gave it to us. We didn't just bring it out, it was sent down. The latest theory indeed says that and we believe in The Qur'an without scientific theories being updated and changed, Allah S.W.T told us that this element is a special element that I have given. There are so many other examples in The Qur'an about water cycle, vegetation going on Earth, the mountains giving stability to the Earth. So many miracles that scientific miracles of The Qur'an literally is an indication that this is a book that has come from Allah S.W.T.

THE
CONSOLATION OF
THE QUR'AN

Yet another miracle of The Qur'an is a very strange one. As of this miracle, many of us appreciate it but we don't realise it's a miracle and that is the effect that the Qur'an has on those who listened to it. The fact that The Qur'an has on those who listened to it. It is unbelievable that this book can be heard by those who don't even speak the language. And yet it moves them to tears. Many of us do not speak the Arabic language and yet when The Qur'an is recited, our imaan (faith) goes up, we feel humbled, we feel the awe of the Qur'an. It is a feeling that is not describable.

Many of us don't speak Arabic, but when we're standing behind the imam and he's reciting the Qur'an and for some strange reason, we understand that these are verses pertaining to mercy or these are the verses pertaining to Jannah and these are the verses pertaining to fire of hell. We somehow know this and all of us are a witness to that. Was there once upon a time, we remember clearly standing behind the imam and knowing subconsciously, without knowing how; that these are the verses of mercy and they're making me feel optimistic? These are the verses of punishment and they're making me scared of the punishment of Allah.

It is unexplainable the effect that The Qur'an has on its listeners and once we understand the Qur'an, subhanallah (glory be to Allah), a whole vista of learning, a whole window of understanding and profundity opens up right in front of us. When the Qur'an is recited, it brings grown men to tears, sobbing, because of this voice, this recitation. What other recitation can do this? When somebody listens to Shakespeare, does he start crying? Does he suddenly start going up and down on his emotion? When somebody listens to any language he doesn't understand, is he affected? Nothing affects a person like the Qur'an.

This is exactly what Allah S.W.T mentions in the Qur'an that when they listen to the Qur'an, "When they listen to what has been revealed to the Rasool (Prophet) and they have imaan, Allah says "Their eyes well up in tears". Allah says this of non-muslim, they began to cry because they realise, this is the truth. (Surah Al-Maidah: Verse 83). The very fact that the Qur'an has such a profound impact on those who listened to it, is clearly a miracle. And this is something we don't need to be like an Arabic speaker. When somebody wants to know the miracle of The Qur'an, show him a video of somebody making tilawah (recitation), choose any famous qira'at (reciter); and ask him, does this sound something that any human being can produce?

There is a story of a Christian man who was interested in Islam. He was a music major, he knew music inside and out. He loved melody, he majored in music. He was studying music in university; that was his major. He was given a CD of the Qur'an and was put on for him to listen to. His head just went down and his eyes closed and tears were glistening there and he listened and listened. When it finished, he goes "I don't have words to describe what I just heard. That was amazing. I have never heard anything like this." This is exactly what Allah says in The Qur'an, they can't even comprehend the emotions that come forth when they listen to The Qur'an.

THE CERTAINTY OF THE QUR'AN

The following point of the miracle of The Qur'an is the lack of contradiction in it. The Qur'an does not contradict itself. Never does it contradict itself, despite the fact that any book written over a period of 23 years tattering to a myriad of situation, solving legal and theological and political and social problem; must, if it is a human product, have contradiction. Not the Qur'an. Allah says in The Qur'an,

> "Don't they think about The Qur'an? Had it been from other than Allah, they would have found much in it to contradict itself."

(Surah *An-Nisa'*: Verse 82)

THE GUARDIANS OF THE QUR'AN

Last discussion of the miracle is one that is very near and dear to all of us and we understand it profoundly. It is one that we experienced, we have witnessed, we know and yet many of us failed to recognize it as a miracle and that is the miracle of the memorization of the Qur'an (Hafizul Qur'an). The memorizing of the Qur'an. Now, there are people who have taught Shakespeare for many years of their life, 30-40 years and yet, they could not repeat a single sonnet in its entirety, word for word, letter for letter.

There are people who have taught a certain book of literature and they know the content inside and out, but they couldn't just close their eyes and begin reciting. Twas the best of times, twas the worst of times, and then they go to the end of the book. They cannot do this. It is humanly impossible to memorize such a large quantity and mass. Not just one person, perhaps we will find a superhuman genius or somebody who has a photographic memory, he memorizes 5 pages, 10 pages and even a hundred pages of The Bible or The Gita, there will only be one in a million. But how about in Islam? What is the percentage of huffaz (Memorizers of Qur'an)? How many huffaz are there?

Every one of us knows plenty of huffaz. We ourselves have memorized portion of the Qur'an.

The Qur'an is a living miracle and we know what makes this miracle even more amazing, mind boggling? It is memorized by people who don't understand a single word of what it means. Imagine ourselves memorizing 10 pages of Chinese language. Imagine memorizing a language we have never heard, read or speak. How would we memorize it? And yet here we have so many people. Not tens, not hundreds, not thousands, not even hundreds of thousands, rather we have millions of Muslims in every single land in every single province in every single city, and we will find hundreds and thousands of people memorizing the entire Qur'an, cover to cover. Word for word, letter for letter, harakah for harakah, sukun for sukun.

If this is not a living miracle, a walking miracle, then by Allah, what is a miracle? What can be bigger than this miracle that a boy of 6 years old, he has memorized the whole Qur'an. There is a man of 66, he has memorized the whole Qur'an. We have met plenty of huffaz and they have memorised the Qur'an wallahi before they could speak even a paragraph of their own language. 5 year old, 6 year old, memorized the whole Qur'an. He can't even speak normally in his own language and yet, he's hafizul Qur'an.

There was a retired elderly man, around 66 years old. He just recently finished memorizing the Qur'an. He began after his retirement. After his retirement, he began memorizing the Qur'an and he's finished. 66 years old! What book can claim this? That no matter what our age is, this is a book, when we read it, when we recite it, it automatically comes into our memory and a person can close his eyes and regurgitate every single word for The Qur'an from memory. This is a living miracle. This is a word of God; speech of Allah.

When we recite the Qur'an, it comes into the heart. It is something that is in entrenched in the heart and Allah mentions this in The Qur'an when He says "These are clear verses that contained in the chest of men who have knowledge." (Surah Al-Ankabut: Verse 49). Allah says, this is a book that will be memorized and kept in their chest. This is exactly what we see around us in every single huffaz of The Qur'an, every single memorizer of The Qur'an, he is a walking and living manifestation of the miracle of The Qur'an.

To conclude this, Allah S.W.T says and let us understand the beauty of why Allah says this, "They ask you for miracles. They want you to bring forth many miracles." Allah says,

"Isn't it a sufficient miracle for them that we have revealed this book that is recited for them? Verily in it, there are signs and tokens for men of understanding."

(Surah *Al-Ankabut*: Verse 51).

In The Qur'an, there is enough of a miracle saying why do we need anything else, this Qur'an is self-sufficient.

Dear brothers and sisters in Islam, we have in our possession the greatest and grandest living miracle that Allah has blessed any prophet with. A concluding parting advice for all of us is to cherish this miracle. Cherish it, love it. Read it, recite it, appreciate the miracle and announce this miracle to the world and when we love the Qur'an and when we show that love to The Qur'an then indeed, Allah S.W.T will bless us through the Qur'an and raise us because of the Qur'an and grant us the 'Izzah (power) and the peace and the honour that we want as a result of our love and dedication to The Qur'an.

The miracles of The Qur'an is endless. We can go on and talk about it. The miracle of The Qur'an is not one point or two point, it is not 10. We can go on talking about the miracle of The Qur'an. However these are only the few miracles and do search for other miracles of the Qur'an.

DISCUSSIONS ON THE MIRACLE OF THE QUR'AN (Q&A)

1. Question (Q):

What is the purpose of repetitiveness of some of the verses in The Qur'an?

Answers (A):

The purpose of repetitiveness or more precisely, the verses are similar because it adds wisdom, structure and further meaning that we don't find in the other similar verse and vice versa. We can learn it further in books of Tafsir where it explains why The Qur'an has chosen one word over the other for respective verses.

2. Question (Q):

The Qur'an should be read with understanding, but nowadays, we hardly see it being understood and put into practice. Is there a suggestion on how to improve this?

Answers (A):

Yes, the least we can do is to read The Qur'an in translation, understand it and implement in it our lives.

This is actually a miracle of The Qur'an that we have undervalued. We have fallen short in life, where we keep The Qur'an only as a family heirloom and at the lowest status in our lives. We overlook that it is actually the book of guidance in life to succeed and not to only be read without acting upon it. When we turn to Allah, He will give us even more and more understanding insya Allah.

3. Question (Q):

There are so many miracle of The Qur'an but why do the unbelievers do not believe in The Qur'an?

Answers (A):

People are not just guided by logic and reason. There is also emotion, pride and adhering with tradition. Anyone studying The Qur'an with an open heart and unbiased mind, will come to the conclusion this is a book from God. Whether he then follows up from the conclusion, he openly accepts Islam or not, that is an internal battle within himself. Nonetheless, we do our best job to convey the truth as much as we can and we leave the hidayah (guidance) to Allah.

GLOSSARY

A.S	: Alaihi Salam - peace be upon him (to other prophets than Prophet Muhammad S.A.W)
Ayat	: Verse (of Qur'an)
Hadith	: A collection of traditions containing sayings of the Prophet Muhammad which, with accounts of his daily practice (the Sunnah), constitute the major source of guidance for Muslims apart from the Qur'an
Hafizul Qur'an	: The guardian or memoriser of the Qur'an
Mu'jizah	: Miracle
Qira'at	: Recitation or reading; the one who recites the Qur'an
Quraish	: 1. Arab people of which Muhammad was a member and which from the 5th century

was distinguished by a religious preeminence associated with its hereditary provision of the pre-Islamic custodians of the Kaaba at Mecca.

2. a member of the Quraish people.

S.A.W. : Sallahualaihi Wa Salam - peace be upon him (Prophet Muhammad S.A.W)

S.W.T. : Subhanahu Wa Ta'ala (Glory to Him - Allah, the Exalted)

Sahih Bukhari : One of the authentic Muslim scholars of the hadith of Prophet Muhammad S.A.W

Salam : Peace

Surah : Chapter (of Qur'an)

Tafsir : Interpretation

Ummah : The whole community of Muslims bound together by ties of religion

NOTES

NOTES